FOUR HOUR MINI BUSINESS PLAN WORKBOOK

Write Your Business Plan in Just 4 Hours!!!

By

Dr. Carol A. Parker

ISBN-13:
978-1548329150

ISBN-10:
1548329150

FOUR-HOUR MINI-BUSINESS PLAN WORKBOOK

The key to the success of any business is to have goals, and an action plan that outlines how you are going to achieve those goals.

Building a business plan can be an intimidating task. Who has the time? Who really needs one since you're self-funding and aren't looking for loans. If you think that you don't need a business plan, you're mistaken. Every company needs to know their vision and mission, some idea of what their selling to their customers, some idea about how they're going to fund the company, etc. ...

Here's a secret though – putting together your basic, workable business plan can take less than 4-hours.

Now, this isn't the plan that's going to garner millions in funding, but it is something that you can accomplish in a short period of time that helps to crystallize your company's vision and mission.

It is something that you can use to make sure that you daily focus on your company / brand. And it is something that you can use every day as a framework for your decision-making process.

A basic business plan needs to be your first step in your business success. It should only take four hours to complete this plan, and at the end you should be able to move forward with your new or existing business idea or to rethink your plan. You then need to regularly track the performance of your business to make ensure you're on track to achieve your goals. If you are not then you will need to make some strategic changes to your business.

This workbook is designed to be general and to apply to most businesses, including network marketing and online web business. Therefore, some of the questions may not apply to your specific business. Please go through the document and answer the questions where necessary. Remember this is your plan and your business. Put your best thoughts and effort into it.

Carol A. Parker, Ed.D.
Entrepreneur, Professor,

Realtor, Author

YOU will write a mini-business plan that creates a new or existing business which will market your product or service. You will need to be familiar with the product or service for which you are writing this business plan. Set aside approximately one hour for each of the four sections of this business plan.

Task: Write a Business Plan describing your company.

Research   Gather the information you need through any of the following means:

Methods:

- Library research
- Database searching
- Personal knowledge
- Interviews
- Surveys
- Other

SECTION ONE: DESCRIBE YOUR BUSINESS – TELL YOUR STORY

- 'Tell Your Story',
- describe your 'Company',
- describe your 'Products/Services',
- validate a 'Need' for your Products/Services

COMPANY:

- **I would like to introduce you to (Name of company)**

  _____
  _____
  _____
  _____
  _____
  _____
  _____

- **located at (your company and address)**

  _____
  _____
  _____
  _____
  _____
  _____
  _____

- The Company will start doing business on
  _____ (Date) and will operate as a
  _____ (Sole
  Proprietorship, Partnership, and Corporation)

- The company will <u>(Sell, import, distribute,
  manufacture, service, etc.)</u> a line of quality
  (Describe your products)

  _____

  _____

  _____

  _____

  _____

  _____

  _____

  _____

  _____

  _____

  _____

  _____

This business is important because

_____

_____

_____

_____
_____
_____
_____
_____
_____
_____
_____
_____
_____
_____
_____
_____
_____

- **Tell your story. (Why this business is important for you to start or grow. How will your products/services help your customer? Describe special opportunities you have, etc.)**

_____
_____
_____
_____
_____
_____
_____

Mission Statement (example)

- _____ will
 distribute/ sell/ manufacture, etc. the
 (Company Name)

 best _____
 available in the market place.
 (Name your products/services)

Your Mission Statement could include references to
customer value, how company values employees,
investors, service, environment, etc.

_____
_____
_____
_____
_____
_____
_____
_____
_____
_____
_____
_____
_____
_____
_____
_____

_____

_____

_____

_____

_____

_____

_____

_____

_____

_____

_____

_____

_____

_____

_____

_____

PRODUCTS or SERVICES:

- I became interested in these product/service ....
  (Do you personally buy or /use similar
  products/services

_____

_____

_____

_____

_____

_____

_____

_____

_____

_____

_____

_____

_____

_____

_____

_____

_____

_____

_____

_____

_____

_____

- Describe your Products/Services

_____

_____

_____

_____

_____

_____

_____

_____

_____

_____

_____

_____

_____

_____

_____

_____

_____

_____

- Describe how your Product/service is Different from the competition. (Look at quality, function, price, customer service, packaging, etc.)

_____

_____

_____

_____

_____

_____

_____

_____

_____

_____

_____

_____

_____

_____

- Describe customer benefits that will help you 'Position' your products/services (reference to higher quality, improved function, longer life, etc.)

_____

_____

_____

_____

_____

_____

_____

_____

_____

_____

_____

_____

_____

_____

_____

_____

_____

_____

SECTION TWO: DESCRIBE YOUR MARKETING STRATEGY

DEVELOP YOUR MARKETING PLAN:

Industry Information and Market Trends

- The company's products/services will compete in a general industry category defined as _____ with _____ SIC Code and _____ NAICS Code
- Sales for these type products/services were $ _____, for _____ (year) and estimated at $ _____ for _____ (year)
- Initial research has verified the opportunities in the marketplace for the company's products/services. (Describe how/if the market needs better quality product/service and how your company will fill this need)

_____

_____

_____

_____

_____

_____

_____

_____

_____

_____

Customers and Target Market

- Research has identified the following demographics for customers that are buying similar products/services.

- Average age _____, Age span is from _____ to _____;

- Gender ____% of sales is to Males, and _____% to Females,

- General occupations are_____,_____,_____,

- Est. Household Income is $ _____,

- Customers generally work in a ____ mile radius and live in a _____ mile radius of the business and general shop within a _____ mile radius of their workplace. Other

_____

_____

_____

_____

_____

_____

_____

_____

_____

_____

_____

_____

_____

_____

_____

_____

_____

_____

_____

_____

_____

_____

_____

- Initially I will assume that my customers will fit this same demographic profile and will track sales for the first year to develop more accurate demographics for the company.

_____

_____

_____

_____

_____

_____

_____

_____

_____

_____

_____

_____

_____

_____

_____

Competition (Also see Products/Services above)

- After studying the marketplace, the company has identified the top two direct competitors and have tried to objectively evaluate their market position.

- No. 1 Competitor_____, _____,
  Rating their products = ___, your products =
  ___

- Company Address Rate product/service on a 1-10 scale with 10 = Great No. 2 Competitor
  _____, _____, Rating their products =
  ___, your products = ___

- Company Address Rate product/service on a 1-10 scale with 10 = Great **Product/Service Niche,**

_____

_____

_____

_____

_____

_____

_____

_____

_____

_____

_____

_____

_____

_____

_____

_____

_____

_____

_____

_____

Position and Differentiation

- In developing the Marketing Plan the company will take advantage of the following product strengths/advantages and will use these to help positioning our product/services.

_____

_____

_____

_____

_____

_____

_____

- Options could include, your quality standard, your value, price, technology, unique design, unique packaging, premium or economy product line, added convenience, strong quality assurance program, strong after sale service, products are easy to find and purchase, convenient distribution, strong product support, etc.

_____

_____

_____

_____

_____

_____

_____

_____

_____

_____

_____

_____

_____

_____

_____

Analyzing the Competition

Understanding who your direct and potential competitors are can reduce the risk of failure for your company. Keep in mind that your operation's competitors could be companies in rival industries producing products or services that fall into another industry category, but that solve the same customer problem. In the process of developing a business plan, you need to evaluate who these rival companies are and how they can have an impact on your company.

Consider your own company when answering the questions below. Doing this will help you to identify your company's competition and emphasize your company's competitive advantages in its business plan.

Determine the level of threat each competitor poses to your operation by answering the questions below:

1. Who are your competitors? (What companies solve the same problem?)

_____

_____

_____

_____

_____
_____
_____
_____
_____
_____
_____
_____
_____
_____
_____
_____
_____
_____
_____
_____
_____
_____

2. What are their products?

_____
_____
_____
_____
_____
_____
_____
_____
_____
_____
_____

_____

_____

_____

_____

_____

3. What are their services?

_____

_____

_____

_____

_____

_____

_____

_____

_____

_____

_____

_____

_____

_____

_____

4. What are their major strengths?

_____

_____

_____

_____

5. What are their major weaknesses?

_____

_____

_____

_____

_____

_____

_____

_____

_____

_____

_____

_____

_____

_____

_____

_____

6. What are their marketing strategies?

_____

_____

_____

_____

_____

_____

_____

_____

_____

_____

_____

_____

_____

_____

_____

7. How much market share does each competitor control?

_____

_____

_____

_____

_____

_____

_____

_____

_____

_____

_____

_____

8. What are their key success factors?

_____

_____

_____

_____

_____

_____

_____

_____

_____

_____

_____

_____

_____

_____

9. What differentiates your product or service from your competitors' products or services? (How are you responding to a customer need in a new, useful, and unique way?)

_____

_____

_____

_____

_____

_____

_____

_____

_____

_____

_____

_____

_____

_____

10. Do they enjoy strong brand recognition of their products or services? Be specific.

_____

_____

_____

_____

_____

_____

_____

_____

_____

_____

_____

_____

_____

11. Will they aggressively block the entrance of your operation?

_____

_____
_____
_____
_____
_____
_____
_____
_____
_____
_____
_____
_____
_____
_____

12. Will they recognize your special differentiating attributes and appropriate them for their own products and services?

_____
_____
_____
_____
_____
_____
_____

Marketing/Sales Tools and Monthly Marketing Budget

- The company will develop a diversified Marketing Plan using most of the marketing tools used by our competitors and outside sales manager.

- Traditional Marketing tools for the first year include- (See list 606 and 606a)

_____

_____

_____

_____

_____

_____

_____

_____

_____

_____

_____

_____

_____

_____

_____

_____

- The company will also supplement these Marketing tools with the following

_____

_____

_____

_____

_____

_____

_____

_____

_____

_____

_____

_____

_____

_____

_____

- To achieve first year Sales goals the company will invest $_____ per month in Marketing/Sales which will equal _____% of est. Sales.

_____

_____

_____

_____

_____

_____

_____

_____

SECTION THREE: Financial Assumptions and Budgets

- Develop **'Financial Assumptions and Budgets'** that will show how you will make money and how much money you will need to start the business and terms for this money.

Financial Plan
- ☐ Financial Analysis
- ☐ Budget
- ☐ Return On Investment
- ☐ Supporting Documents

(P&L statements, balance sheets, cash flow, etc.)

FINANCIAL PLAN

- The company will have the following financial systems in place before starting the business: The initial accounting system will be

  _____.

  (Manual, computer or contract with outside bookkeeping service)

- The company has developed a 'Chart of Accounts' that will provide management information for the following 'Profit Centers'. (Profit Centers could help you track Sales for 'Mail Order, Wholesale, Internet, etc.)

-

- To improve fiscal reliability the company has developed Conservative Budget Assumptions for-
    - Total and Net Sales with Discounts, Returns, etc.,
    - Cost of Goods and Gross Profit
    - Expenses and Net Profit

The Budget Assumptions have helped to develop the following reliable Budgets,

- Monthly Pro Forma Budget for the first year,
- Startup Costs and additional Financing required and
- Monthly Cash Flow Budgets

_____

_____

_____

_____

_____

_____

_____

_____

_____

_____

_____

_____

_____

_____

_____

- Each month the company will compare 'Actual Monthly Income Statement' with 'Monthly Pro Forma Budgets' to help insure the company is 'On Budget'. If there are differences the company will take steps to correct fiscal problems quickly to help Profitability.

- The company will also implement a standard 'Financial Control System' for handling cash, checks, bank deposits, opening mail, etc.

_____

_____

_____

_____

_____

_____

_____

_____

_____

_____

_____

- The 'Financial Plan' should allow the company to 'Break Even' in the first _____ months of Operations and achieve _____% Profit for the first year. (See Pro Forma Budget)

_____

_____

_____

_____

_____

_____

_____

_____

_____

_____

_____

_____

_____

_____

_____

RISK ANALYSIS:

- In conducting the research for the Business Plan the company has identify the following potential Business Risk. (Identify risks that are 'Out of Your Control'. Examples could be Local, State, National Economy, Weather, Starbucks Effect, Higher Cost, etc.)

_____

_____

_____

_____

_____

_____

_____

_____

_____

_____

_____

_____

_____

_____

- The company will reduce, or minimize these risks by

SECTION FOUR: ACTION PLAN –

WHAT WILL YOU DO NOW / TODAY TO MAKE THIS HAPPEN?

Make an Action Plan

This is the number one secret to an effective business plan; regardless of what your plan is, the key to reaching it is always the same. The best, perhaps the only, way to turn your business plan into an attainable reality is to create an action plan; a down to earth, no-nonsense action plan.

The fact is that when business people set measurable goals, they are much more likely to attain them. That means not just defining your objectives, but also defining the resources, time and money you'll need to invest in order to achieve them.

Achieving your goals, even big goals, doesn't require brilliance or talent. It does, however, require determination and tenacity, and most of all, a realistic action plan. If you don't plan, you plan to fail.

Put It in Writing

Every business requires a marketing plan, sales plan, recruitment plan, process plan and financial plan. Note the common word in all this activity: plan. Goals are nothing more than what you "plan" to accomplish.

So, write your goals down. Then, start filling in the blanks between Point A (where you are today) and Point Z (where you want to be). The act of writing your ideas down, or say, keying them into your laptop, will force you to think in concrete terms. It will also spark additional ideas. This is the birth of your action plan.

Be Specific

Break your plan down into baby steps and attach a realistic deadline to each step. Determine how to measure your progress; these measurements will be your reality check.

Then, define your investment. How much will each step cost, in terms of dollars, time, research and energy? What resources can you draw from and what additional resources will you need to acquire?

Eventually, you will have a full-blown action plan. Don't tuck it in a drawer--keep it close by for constant reference. Make regular appointments with yourself to review your plan and ensure you stay on track. It is a work-in-progress, and you can expect to make changes as you proceed. That's okay, just don't stop working on it.

Remember, there's only one way to eat an elephant: one bite at a time.

Create Your Timeline

Your final step is to create a timeline to your action plan. It helps to rough in the timeline on a monthly basis at first and then refine it as time progresses.

Once the timeline is created your action plan can be used as a checklist to ensure that you actually do the things you wrote about in your business plan. You have turned a theoretical document into a powerful business compass.

Here is an excerpt of a sample timeline based on a semi-final marketing plan:

Marketing Plan: Semi-Final List	Completed
Month	**Marketing / Sales Activities**
June	**Develop materials**
June 1	Join industry association (sign-up online)
June 1 - 10	Write sales letter, create brochure
June 10	Print sample 50 brochures
June 15	Morning networking (bring brochures)
June 11 - 20	Input 500 contacts into contact management software (Act, Goldmine, etc.)
July 14-28	Interview & hire telemarketer
June 22	First mailing
July	**Start calling**
July 2-10	Input 500 more contacts
July 2	Start cold-calling
July 17	Networking (bring brochures)
July 24	Second mailing
August	**Refinement**
August 2-10	Input 500 more contacts
August 2	Continue cold-calling
August 14	Networking (bring brochures)
August 21	Second mailing

AND LAST, BUT NOT LEAST -

NOW that you have completed your 4-Hour Business Plan Workbook there is still some actions you must take.

1. Reserve your business name through your state.gov business registration site

2. Obtain an Employer Identification Number (EIN) from the www.irs.gov website

3. Decide what kind of business form you want to be – Sole proprietor, Corporation, S-corporation, LLC, etc. (research each type before assuming what is best for you and your business)

4. Register your business through your state.gov business registration site

5. Obtain a domain name similar to or the same as your registered business name.

6. Open a business account at your bank or credit union. They will be happy to help you.

7. Obtain a business permit or license from your local city or county government, if required.

8. Establish a website or blog that will help you market your business. Social media sites have a

variety of choices for you. Choose the one (or 2) that you are most comfortable using.

9. Establish a regular schedule for your work at a time when you can *focus* without distractions.

10. Start your marketing campaign and start generating income.

Welcome to Small Business and Entrepreneurship!

www.ingramcontent.com/pod-product-compliance
Lightning Source LLC
Chambersburg PA
CBHW051238170526
45165CB00004B/1487